BAN THIS BOOK NOW!

BAN THIS BOOK NOW!

THE POLITICS AND POWER OF BOOK BANS

Cara Cusack

CaraCusackBooks.com

Contents

1

Introduction

Ladies and gentlemen, prepare yourselves for a book so danger-ous, so provocative, and so subversive that it should be banned from every shelf, burned in bonfires, and kept hidden away from innocent eyes. Yes, we are diving headfirst into a whirlwind of topics that some deem too uncomfortable, too sensitive, and dare I say, too enlightening.

Why should we bother educating ourselves about the uncom-fortable realities of book bans? Why expose our children to the audacity of critical thinking and independent thought? Isn't it better to shield them from the inconvenient truths of history, like the atrocities of slavery, women's rights, or the Holocaust? After all, that will just hurt their feelings and who needs a well-rounded education when we can just keep them safely ignorant?

Why should we let our precious little ones be burdened by the knowledge of the struggles faced by women throughout history? Why should they be subjected to the radical notion that women are capable of shaping the world around them? Why on earth should we allow our innocent darlings to be traumatized by reading about exploring their own sexual identity? Why expose them to the realities of a diverse and complex world? Let's just stick to comfortable fairy tales and keep them safely confined to traditional gender roles, shall we? After all, a child won't know they are gay if we don't let them know the possibility exists, right? Let's just keep them sheltered and protected from such confusion.

After all, what harm could it possibly do to shield our children from the harsh realities of life and our own history? Let's just pretend that the world is all rainbows and unicorns, where everyone is treated fairly and no one faces discrimination or adversity. Who needs empathy, resilience, or an understanding of social issues anyway?

Who needs diversity, inclusivity, and acceptance when we can enforce our own narrow worldview onto the minds of young, impressionable children? Why should we allow them to think for themselves and form their own opinions? How will we entomb our own religious beliefs on them if they are taught the ability to question? It's much better for us, the ones who are right, to enforce our own religious and moral beliefs onto all children, regardless of what their parents may want for them. We know better than those progressive thinkers anyway. After all, the concept of critical thinking and open-mindedness is overrated. Let's keep our children sheltered from any information that might challenge their beliefs or broaden their perspectives. Ignorance is bliss, right?

If we allow other people's children to explore different ideas and encounter people who are different from us, who knows what could happen when our own children are exposed to such things?

They could develop empathy, compassion, and understanding or even learn to respect and appreciate individuals who don't conform to our limited worldview. And who wants that?

By suppressing the truth and limiting their exposure to diverse perspectives, we can ensure that our society remains stagnant and closed off from progress. We need a society where ignorance reigns supreme and fear of the unknown governs our actions. After all, why should we strive for a society that embraces diversity, promotes equality, and fosters understanding? That would be far too challenging and disruptive.

So, let's continue to enforce our beliefs on other people's children because, clearly, our perspective is the only valid one. Let's preserve a world where conformity trumps individuality and ignorance triumphs over knowledge. Who needs an enlightened and inclusive society when we can live in a bubble of self-righteousness and ignorance?

Maintaining a population that is uneducated and easily manipulated is key to preserving our power and advancing our own agendas. Why would we want an informed electorate that questions our policies and holds us accountable? They might even vote and then what will happen to us?

By keeping our children sheltered from different perspectives, we can shape their minds to align with our own conservative ideals. We can instill in them the belief that enriching corporations and protecting the interests of the wealthy are the only paths to prosperity. After all, who needs social equality and a fair distribution of resources when we can ensure that the poor remain poor and uneducated?

Our religious beliefs serve as a convenient tool to control the masses and we should use that to our advantage. By indoctrinating our children with religious teachings, we can instill in them a sense of unquestioning obedience and blind faith. They will grow up believing that our policies and actions are divinely sanctioned, further solidifying our hold on power.

An uneducated and easily swayed population is far less likely to challenge the norm. By limiting their exposure to different ideas, critical thinking, and diverse perspectives, we can ensure that they remain loyal followers, blindly supporting our conservative agenda without question.

Let's face it, an educated and informed society poses a threat to the power and control of our children and communities. We must keep the masses in ignorance and manipulate their beliefs to maintain our dominance. After all, why would we want an empowered population capable of making independent decisions and demanding accountability from their leaders?

So it is essential for us to continue to withhold knowledge, suppress dissent, and perpetuate inequality. By doing so, we can secure our own dominance and encapsulate a system that benefits us and our corporate allies at the expense of the marginalized and disadvantaged. After all, ignorance is the key to control, and control is the key to maintaining our power.

In the pages that follow, we dare to shine a light on the uncomfortable – our brutal history and the dark secrets that have plagued humanity. We spare no expense in unraveling the threads of society's deepest taboos. Brace yourselves, for we shall venture into the treacherous territories of slavery, racism, sexism, substance abuse, and those oh-so-scandalous matters of sexual well-being, identity and puberty.

Now, why on earth would anyone in their right mind choose to explore these forbidden topics? It's simple really, we need to understand why these books have been banned and how it affects future generations.

So, my dear readers, be prepared to have your fragile sensibilities shattered, your preconceived notions challenged, and your comfort zones obliterated. This book should be banned, not because it spreads hate or promotes violence, but because it dares to ask uncomfortable questions and confronts the realities that make us squirm in our seats.

But remember, knowledge is a dangerous thing, so after I explain why all of these books must be banned, you will have to ban this book as well because it will hold all of the secrets our children could use as adults to undo all the hard work we put into suppressing them. Are you brave enough to embrace it and hold this knowledge hostage?

2

The Art of Ignorance

We have all seen the recent news about the banning of books in schools and public libraries, but do you know where they started? Book banning is an ancient practice, with its roots reaching back to the dawn of written text. One of the earliest recorded instances comes from 213 BCE, during the reign of China's first emperor, Qin Shi Huang. As a part of his effort to consolidate power and standardize thought, Huang ordered the burning of historical and philosophical texts, marking the beginning of a long tradition of suppressing knowledge for control.

In the Middle Ages, the Catholic Church emerged as another formidable player in the world of book banning. They created the 'Index Librorum Prohibitorum,' or 'Index of Forbidden Books,' which listed texts deemed heretical, anti-clerical, or lascivious, and thus forbidden to its followers. The Index was active from 1559 to 1966 and included works from notable authors like Galileo Galilei and Johannes Kepler.

The Nazi regime in Germany orchestrated extensive book burnings in the 1930s. This campaign targeted materials considered "un-German," particularly focusing on works written by Jewish authors or those presenting views contrary to Nazi ideology.

It was Adolf Hitler who said, "*He who owns the youth owns the future.*"

In the United States, the second half of the 20th century saw an increase in book bans and challenges, often rooted in the desire to shield young readers from perceived inappropriate content. This sentiment led to the challenges against and bans of many classic novels considered literary greats.

In the 21st century, the reasons for book banning have continued to evolve and reflect contemporary societal and political issues. A survey conducted by PEN America between July and December 2022 reveals an unsettling trend of growing censorship in the United States. The data shows that the trend has its epicenter in the southern states and is particularly focused on content related to race and sexuality, with LGBTQ+ themes being a notable target.

In this recent wave, more than hundreds of unique titles have been challenged or banned, amounting to a 67% increase over the previous year. The highest numbers of bans were seen in Texas, Florida, and Missouri. The most commonly challenged themes were LGBTQ+ content, Critical Race Theory, sex education, and politics & government.

We have also seen legislation playing an increasingly significant role in book banning, with numerous states passing laws that restrict certain types of content. For example, in Florida, the "Parental Rights in Education Act" or the "Don't Say Gay" law, led to the removal of several books with LGBTQ+ content from school libraries. In Utah, the "Sensitive Materials in Schools" law resulted in the removal of works containing sexual content. In Missouri, a provision in S.B. 775 led to the removal of several graphic novels deemed "harmful to minors".

Legislation in other states like Tennessee, Georgia, and Arizona introduced new processes for evaluating book challenges, which potentially increase the likelihood of book bans. This trend has resulted in what PEN America calls "wholesale bans," where entire classrooms and school libraries have been emptied of books due to fears of legal repercussions.

As we look hard into the reasons behind this surge in book bans, it is clear that political, social, and religious motives often underpin these actions. It is important to analyze these motives in greater detail, shedding light on the various forces driving this modern wave of censorship.

The practice of banning books often mirrors societal fears, insecurities, and the desire to control the narrative. It highlights an ongoing struggle between the pursuit of knowledge and the comfort of ignorance, the tension between freedom of expression and the impulse to suppress. These debates surrounding book bans continue to shape discussions about education, literature, and societal norms.

The surge in bans in the United States between 2021-2023 is symptomatic of a larger sociopolitical landscape marked by contentious debate and polarization. Understanding the motives requires an exploration of the intersecting political, social, and religious factors at play.

These bans not only limit the diversity of content accessible to students but also preemptively decide what's suitable for them to read. This essentially strips parents of the opportunity to make informed decisions about their children's reading material based on their individual maturity and understanding.

Many of the books that have fallen victim to bans will fit into more than one category and while discussing every banned book would be an insurmountable task, I will explore a selection of notable and surprising examples, categorizing them to the best of my ability.

3

Erasing History and Racial Bias

Books have always played a crucial role in preserving our collective history, shedding light on the struggles, triumphs, and atrocities that have shaped our society. However, there have been instances where books delving into historical atrocities have faced censorship and bans. These bans often stem from the belief among conservatives that such books may make white children feel uncomfortable or guilty about the past.

While these concerns may arise from a desire to protect young minds, it is essential to recognize that understanding and learning from our past is vital for personal growth and societal progress. Banning historical books and books that address racial diversity not only limits the education of all students but also hinders our ability to collectively grow and strive for a more inclusive and just society.

Throughout history, numerous books addressing significant historical events, such as slavery, the Holocaust, and civil rights movements, have been subjected to censorship and bans. These books offer invaluable perspectives on our shared history, providing opportunities for critical engagement, empathy, and dialogue. By examining these cases, we can gain insight into the reasons behind these bans and the impact they have on our understanding of the past.

"The Life of Rosa Parks" by Kathleen Connors is a biographical book that tells the story of Rosa Parks, a civil rights activist known for her pivotal role in the Montgomery Bus Boycott. Her refusal to give up her seat to a white passenger on a segregated bus sparked a major movement against racial segregation in the United States. However, despite the historical significance and the lessons it offers about the struggle for civil rights, this book has faced censorship in certain educational settings, erasing the invaluable contributions and sacrifices made by individuals like Rosa Parks.

"Who was Sojourner Truth?" by Yona Zeldis McDonough and Who HQ is a children's biography that introduces young readers to the remarkable life of abolitionist and women's rights activist, Sojourner Truth. She played a pivotal role in the fight against slavery and advocated for gender equality. Yet, despite her important place in history, this book has been subjected to bans, depriving students of the opportunity to learn about her remarkable journey and the legacy she left behind.

"Nelson Mandela" by Kadir Nelson is about, the renowned South African anti-apartheid revolutionary and political leader, who dedicated his life to fighting against racial segregation and advocating

for equality and justice. His biography serves as an inspiration to many, offering valuable insights into the struggle against oppression. The banning of this biography in certain educational contexts limits students' understanding of his remarkable achievements and the ongoing fight for social justice.

"*Maus*" by Art Spiegelman is a graphic novel that tells the story of the Holocaust through the experiences of the author's father, a Holocaust survivor. It portrays Jews as mice and Nazis as cats, using allegory to depict the horrors of the Holocaust. Despite its critical acclaim and widespread recognition as an important work of literature, it has been the target of book bans due to its explicit content and controversial imagery. The censorship of "Maus" not only restricts students' access to a profound historical narrative but also undermines the power of art and storytelling in conveying the human experience during a dark chapter in history.

"*The Color Purple*" by Alice Walker is a Pulitzer Prize-winning novel that explores the lives of African American women in the early 20th century. It tackles themes of racism, sexism, and oppression, portraying the experiences of black women within a context of systemic injustice. Despite its critical acclaim and literary significance, it has faced challenges and bans in schools due to its explicit content, including depictions of sexual abuse and violence.

"*Roots*" by Alex Haley is a groundbreaking work of historical fiction that traces the author's family history back to Africa and chronicles the journey of African Americans through slavery and its aftermath. It provides a comprehensive account of the brutal realities of slavery and the resilience of those who endured it. However, it has been targeted for censorship, with challenges raised against its portrayal of violence, sexual content, and racial themes.

"To Kill a Mockingbird" by Harper Lee is a classic novel that confronts racial injustice and prejudice in the Deep South during the 1930s. Through the eyes of Scout Finch, the story explores themes of racism, social inequality, and the loss of innocence. Despite its status as a literary masterpiece, it has faced numerous challenges and bans for its use of racial slurs and its depiction of sensitive subjects related to race.

"Things Fall Apart" by Chinua Achebe is a seminal novel that portrays the life of Okonkwo, an Igbo warrior in pre-colonial Nigeria, and the impact of British colonialism on his community. It examines themes of cultural clash, colonialism, and the erosion of traditional values. Despite its critical acclaim and cultural significance, it has been subject to bans and challenges, with objections raised against its portrayal of African culture and colonial history.

"A Lesson Before Dying" by Ernest J. Gaines is a powerful novel that explores racial injustice and the dehumanizing impact of the criminal justice system in 1940s Louisiana. The story revolves around a young black man wrongly convicted of murder and his relationship with a teacher who helps him find dignity and purpose. Despite its acclaim and recognition as an important work of literature, it has faced challenges and bans due to its racial themes and language.

"Beloved" by Toni Morrison is a haunting and critically acclaimed novel that delves into the legacy of slavery and its profound impact on individuals and communities. Through the story of Sethe, a former slave, Morrison explores themes of memory, trauma, and

the search for freedom and identity. Despite its literary accolades, it has been frequently challenged and banned for its explicit content, including depictions of violence, sexual abuse, and its unflinching portrayal of the horrors of slavery.

"Invisible Man" by Ralph Ellison is a landmark novel that explores the experiences of an African American man navigating racism and invisibility in a racially divided society. It addresses themes of identity, social invisibility, and the complexities of racial identity and self-perception. Despite its significance in African American literature, it has faced challenges and bans due to its explicit content, political themes, and discussions of race and power dynamics.

"Black Boy" by Richard Wright is a memoir that chronicles the author's experiences growing up in the segregated South and his journey toward self-discovery and intellectual liberation. It explores themes of racism, poverty, and the pursuit of education as a means of empowerment. Despite its literary merit and its role as a valuable historical document, it has been challenged and banned for its depiction of racial violence and its frank discussions of racism.

"The Bluest Eye" by Toni Morrison is a novel that examines issues of beauty, race, and identity through the story of a young black girl named Pecola Breedlove. It delves into the destructive effects of internalized racism and societal beauty standards. Despite its critical acclaim, it has faced bans and challenges due to its explicit content, including scenes of sexual violence and discussions of sensitive subjects related to race and identity.

"The Autobiography of Malcolm X" by Malcolm X and Alex Haley is a seminal work that documents the life and transformation of

civil rights activist Malcolm X. It explores themes of racial identity, self-discovery, and the struggle for justice and equality. Despite its historical significance and influence, it has faced challenges and bans for its frank discussions of race, religion, and political ideologies.

"I Know Why the Caged Bird Sings" by Maya Angelou is the first volume of Maya Angelou's acclaimed autobiographical series. It recounts her childhood experiences, including the challenges of racism, trauma, and the power of literature as a means of self-expression and resilience. Despite its literary acclaim and recognition as an important work of African American literature, it has faced bans and challenges for its depictions of sensitive subjects, including sexual abuse and racism.

"The 1619 Project" by Nikole Hannah-Jones is a groundbreaking and thought-provoking book that challenges our understanding of American history. By revisiting the nation's past and exploring the legacy of slavery and anti-Black racism, Hannah-Jones sheds light on the enduring issues of race and inequality that persist in our society today. Despite being banned in some school districts, this book is a crucial contribution to both Black history and American history, inviting readers to confront uncomfortable truths and engage in meaningful conversations about our collective past and present. It is a must-read for anyone seeking a deeper understanding of the complexities of race in America.

"Dad, Jackie and Me" is a children's book that tells the story of Jackie Robinson, the renowned baseball player, and the discrimination he encountered as a black man breaking the color barrier in Major League Baseball. This inspiring tale also addresses the prejudices faced by deaf individuals, offering a powerful message of

overcoming adversity and promoting inclusivity. Through its engaging narrative, young readers are introduced to important themes of racial equality and understanding, as well as the importance of embracing diversity in society.

"Antiracist Baby" by Ibram X. Kendi is an empowering book that aims to teach children and readers of all ages the importance of actively opposing racism. With its engaging illustrations and simple yet impactful text, the book guides readers through key concepts and actions that foster an antiracist mindset. It encourages readers to examine their own beliefs, biases, and privileges, and to actively challenge and dismantle systemic racism. By promoting self-reflection, empathy, and taking a stand against injustice, it serves as a powerful tool for cultivating a more inclusive and equitable society.

"Running the Road to ABC" by Denize Lauture is a vibrant and beautifully illustrated picture book that takes readers on a captivating journey alongside six Haitian children as they make their way to school. From the early hours of the morning, even before the sun has risen, these enthusiastic students embark on an adventurous trek, traversing hills, fields, and the bustling city square. Guided by the warmth of the morning sun and the melodies of nature, they eagerly navigate their nation's picturesque landscapes, all in pursuit of knowledge. This enchanting story celebrates the importance of literacy, resilience, and the transformative power of education, offering readers a glimpse into the lives and experiences of Haitian children.

"The Hill We Climb: An Inaugural Poem for the Country" by Amanda Gorman is a poignant and inspiring work that marked a historic

moment in American literature. On January 20, 2021, Gorman, at the young age of 22, captivated the world with her powerful recitation as the sixth and youngest poet to perform at a presidential inauguration. Following the 46th president of the United States, Joe Biden, Gorman's words resonated deeply, instilling a sense of unity and optimism in the hearts of viewers worldwide. This extraordinary poem not only celebrates the promise of America but also reaffirms the transformative power of poetry in shaping our collective consciousness. It is a testament to the enduring spirit of hope and the capacity of words to inspire positive change.

"Cows for America" by Carmen Agra Deedy is a New York Times bestseller that recounts a heartwarming true story following the September 11 attacks. In a remote village in western Kenya, an extraordinary ceremony takes place in June 2002, just nine months after the devastating event. Surrounded by hundreds of Maasai people, an American diplomat is there to accept an unexpected and touching gift from these legendary Maasai warriors. The gift, fourteen cows, symbolizes hope and friendship for a grieving American nation, shining a light in the midst of darkness and offering solace in the face of tragedy.

"Black Frontiers: A History of African American Heroes in the Old West" by Lillian Schlissel, takes readers back in time to the period between 1865 and the early 1900s when courageous black individuals embarked on a journey westward, seeking a new life for themselves and their families. These pioneers ventured into unfamiliar territories as scouts, mountain men, miners, homesteaders, soldiers, business owners, and cowboys.

"Carter Reads the Newspaper" by Deborah Hopkinson presents the first-ever picture book biography of Carter G. Woodson, renowned as the Father of Black History Month. From his childhood as the son of formerly enslaved parents to his impactful role in promoting the history of African Americans, Woodson's passion for knowledge and education shines through. The book highlights Woodson's dedication to being an informed citizen and his commitment to researching and sharing the stories of his people. Inspired by a coal miner named Oliver Jones, young Carter takes on the task of reading to his fellow miners and delving deeper into subjects that captivate their interest.

"The Color of My Words" by Lynn Joseph is a powerful and lyrical novel that explores a young girl's struggle to find her place in the world and pursue her passion for writing. Set in the Dominican Republic, the story intricately weaves poetry and prose as the protagonist navigates a society where words are feared. The novel is an evocative journey into the landscape and culture of the Dominican Republic, capturing the challenges and triumphs of a young girl determined to make her voice heard.

"Climbing Lincoln's Steps: The African American Journey" by Suzanne Slade is an empowering and emotionally charged story that sheds light on significant moments in African American history connected to the Lincoln Memorial. From iconic civil rights activists to President Abraham Lincoln's role in abolishing slavery, this book explores the hardships and triumphs experienced in the fight for racial equality in America. By delving into the struggles and achievements of African Americans, it offers a deeper understanding of the ongoing journey toward justice and equality.

"The ABCs of Black History" by Rio Cortez is a children's book that takes readers on a captivating journey, letter by letter, through the rich tapestry of Black history. From triumph to heartbreak, creativity to joy, the book explores significant moments and iconic figures that have shaped the story of Black people across continents and centuries. Each letter represents a powerful concept or a renowned individual, highlighting the immense contributions and resilience of the Black community.

"One Green Apple" by Eve Bunting tells the poignant story of Farah, a young Muslim immigrant who feels isolated as a new student in school. Struggling with language barriers and a sense of loneliness, she finds solace during a class trip to an apple orchard. As she participates in making apple cider and discovers familiar sounds and moments that connect her to her home country, she begins to forge connections with her classmates and gradually feels a sense of belonging. This timely and heartfelt tale, beautifully illustrated by Ted Lewin, explores themes of empathy, understanding, and finding common ground amidst differences.

"Dreamers" by Yuyi Morales is a stunningly illustrated and deeply resonant book that chronicles the author's own journey as an immigrant to the United States. Bringing her hopes, passion, strength, and stories with her, Morales portrays the power of resilience, dreams, and the human spirit. The book celebrates the idea of making a home wherever one carries their dreams and history, even in unfamiliar surroundings. It is a testament to the courage and determination of immigrants and a reminder that better tomorrows can be built even in challenging times.

"Before She Was Harriet" by Lesa Cline-Ransome is a captivating picture book that pays tribute to the remarkable life of Harriet Tubman. Through evocative poetry and stunning watercolor illustrations, the book explores the different roles and names by which Tubman was known throughout her lifetime. From being a Union spy named General Tubman to leading countless individuals to freedom as Moses on the Underground Railroad, Tubman's indomitable spirit and unwavering commitment to justice and freedom shine through. This beautifully crafted biography celebrates Tubman's enduring legacy as a heroic figure in American history.

"Dumpling Soup" by Jama Kim Rattigan is a heartwarming tale set in the Hawaiian islands that celebrates the joy of family, food, and cultural diversity. The story revolves around Marisa, who gets the opportunity to help make dumplings for the New Year's celebration. However, she worries that her dumplings, with their unique appearance, may not be well-received. The book explores the beauty of mixed families, embracing customs and languages from various cultures.

While these examples are not a complete list, they illustrate how books that provide essential perspectives on historical atrocities, such as slavery and the Holocaust, have been subjected to censorship. By banning books like these, we limit students' access to diverse perspectives and critical discussions about historical events. It is crucial to recognize the detrimental impact of these bans on educational and intellectual growth, as well as the preservation of historical memory.

This not only limits students' access to knowledge but also promotes selective amnesia. By erasing these narratives from educational settings, we hinder the development of a comprehensive understanding of history and its impact on present-day society. Students are denied the opportunity to engage with the complex and often uncomfortable aspects of our shared past, hindering their ability to critically analyze and learn from historical events. In doing this, we suppress open dialogue and hinder the process of reconciliation and societal progress. Understanding and acknowledging past injustices are crucial for fostering empathy, promoting tolerance, and working towards a more inclusive and equitable future.

4

Erasing Identity

Throughout history, books addressing the sensitive topics of sexual identity and LGBTQ+ issues have faced numerous challenges and censorship. These narratives provide crucial insights into the experiences of marginalized individuals, fostering empathy and understanding among readers. However, conservative opposition and concerns about age-appropriateness have led to attempts to silence these important voices. It is important to evaluate the dangers of suppressing these narratives and highlight the need for understanding and acceptance.

These books play a vital role in representing diverse identities and fostering understanding among readers. They provide much-needed visibility to LGBTQ+ individuals, especially young people who are navigating their own identities. However, conservative groups and individuals who oppose LGBTQ+ rights often seek to suppress these narratives, claiming that they promote "alternative lifestyles" or go against their religious beliefs.

"The Story of Harvey Milk" by Kari Krakow is a book that chronicles the life and legacy of Harvey Milk, one of the first openly gay elected officials in the United States. Milk became a prominent LGBTQ+ rights activist and made significant contributions to advancing the rights and visibility of the queer community. However, this book has faced bans due to its LGBTQ+ content, denying students the opportunity to learn about the historical struggles and triumphs of the LGBTQ+ rights movement.

"Call Me Max" by Kyle Lukoff is a children's book that shares the story of Max, a transgender boy, as he navigates his journey of self-discovery and acceptance. It has faced challenges and bans from conservative groups who oppose its portrayal of transgender experiences, arguing that it promotes gender confusion or goes against traditional gender norms.

"King and the Dragonflies" by Kacen Callender is a middle-grade novel that revolves around Kingston, a young boy grappling with grief, friendship, and his exploration of his sexual orientation. It has encountered attempts at censorship due to its portrayal of LGBTQ+ themes. Critics claim that it promotes a "homosexual agenda" or exposes young readers to content they consider inappropriate.

"The Poet X" by Elizabeth Acevedo is a novel-in-verse that follows Xiomara Batista, an Afro-Latina girl who discovers her passion for poetry and challenges the expectations set by her religious family. It gets into themes of self-expression, identity, and sensitive topics such as sexuality and sexual awakening. It has faced bans and challenges for its portrayal of sexuality and its exploration of sensitive subjects.

"Gender Queer" by Maia Kobabe is a graphic memoir that offers an intimate exploration of the author's personal journey and understanding of their gender identity as a non-binary person. It has encountered bans and challenges due to its explicit discussions of gender dysphoria and exploration of non-binary identities. Critics argue that the book promotes confusion or goes against traditional gender norms.

"Flamer" by Mike Curato is a young adult novel that describes the experiences of Aiden, a gay teenager, as he confronts homophobia, and bullying, and seeks self-acceptance. It tackles themes of identity, sexuality, and the impact of internalized homophobia. The book has faced bans and challenges for its frank discussions of sexuality and depiction of same-sex relationships.

"Tricks" by Ellen Hopkins is a young adult novel that interweaves the stories of five teenagers who find themselves involved in prostitution. It addresses themes of sexual exploitation, drug abuse, and the harsh realities faced by vulnerable youth. It has faced bans and challenges due to its explicit content and sensitive subject matter.

"Milk and Honey" by Rupi Kaur is a poetry collection that explores themes of love, loss, trauma, and healing. It has faced bans and challenges for its explicit discussions of sexual experiences and its depiction of sensitive topics such as abuse and violence.

"And Tango Makes Three" by Justin Richardson and Peter Parnell is based on a true story. This picture book introduces readers to two male penguins in the Central Park Zoo who form a same-sex relationship and raise a chick together. It has faced bans and

challenges for its portrayal of same-sex relationships and has been deemed "inappropriate" for young readers by some critics.

"Heather Has Two Mommies" by Lesléa Newman is a children's book that tells the story of Heather, a young girl with two mothers, and celebrates diverse family structures. It has encountered bans and challenges for its portrayal of same-sex parenting. Critics argue that it goes against their beliefs or promotes non-traditional family values.

"In Our Mothers' House" by Patricia Polacco is a picture book that depicts a diverse family with two mothers and their three adopted children, celebrating love, acceptance, and the importance of family. It has faced bans and challenges for its portrayal of same-sex relationships and has been deemed inappropriate or contrary to certain religious beliefs by some individuals.

"All Boys Aren't Blue" by George M. Johnson is a memoir-manifesto that explores the author's life from childhood to his early adult life as a Black queer man in America. The book addresses complex topics such as gender identity, toxic masculinity, brotherhood, family, structural marginalization, consent, and Black joy. It has been banned and challenged due to its explicit content related to sexual orientation, gender identity, and discussions of racism.

"This Book Is Gay" by Juno Dawson is an informative resource and guide about sexuality and gender identity. It is intended to educate and support young adults and teens who are exploring their sexuality or gender, and it includes personal anecdotes, factual information, and supportive advice. The book has been banned or

challenged in some areas due to its explicit discussion of LGBTQ+ topics and sexual content.

"Drama" by Raina Telgemeier is a graphic novel that tells the story of Callie, a middle-schooler and theater enthusiast who works in her school's drama production crew. The novel explores themes of friendship, crushes, and the everyday ups and downs of middle school life. It includes characters who are openly gay and it's their positive representation that has led to the book being banned or challenged in several states, due to objections over content considered inappropriate.

"Beyond Magenta: Transgender Teens Speak Out" by Susan Kuklin is a non-fiction work that includes the personal stories of six transgender or gender-neutral young adults. The author interviewed these individuals and allowed them to share their personal journeys about realizing their true identities and starting the transitioning process. Each individual story paints a portrait of unique experiences and challenges. It has been banned or challenged in several states due to its frank discussions of sexuality, gender identity, and explicit language or scenes considered inappropriate.

"George" by Alex Gino tells the story of a fourth-grade student who, despite being biologically male, identifies as a girl. The main character, George, wishes to play Charlotte in the school's production of "Charlotte's Web," seeing it as an opportunity to reveal her true identity to her family and friends. The novel sensitively explores the experience of a young transgender girl coming to terms with her identity. The book has been banned or challenged in several states for its portrayal of transgender issues and for addressing complex gender identities that some believe are unsuitable.

"It Feels Good to Be Yourself" by Theresa Thorn is an insightful children's book that presents an understanding of gender identity in an accessible way to young readers. It acknowledges that individuals can identify as boys, girls, both, neither, or somewhere in between. The book uses age-appropriate language and vivid artwork to facilitate discussions about this important topic. However, due to its focus on gender identity, a subject that some consider too complex for the target age group, the book has faced bans and challenges in certain areas.

"Julián Is a Mermaid" by Jessica Love is a children's book about Julián, a young boy, who becomes enchanted with the idea of transforming himself into a mermaid. He uses items around his house to create his own fabulous mermaid costume. This book is a celebration of self-expression and individuality. Despite its powerful message, it has been controversial and even banned in some regions due to its implicit depiction of non-traditional gender roles.

"Neither" by Airlie Anderson is a children's book of fiction where in a world populated by blue bunnies and yellow birds, an unusual green creature emerges, one that doesn't fit into any established categories. This creature, known as Neither, embarks on a journey in search of acceptance and discovers a diverse world where all creatures coexist peacefully. The story emphasizes the importance of diversity and inclusion, but it has faced controversy and even bans due to its allegorical representation of non-binary or non-conforming gender identities.

Each of these books has faced opposition from individuals or groups who deem their content inappropriate or contrary to their beliefs. However, proponents of these books argue that they provide important representation, promote understanding, and offer support to readers who may be grappling with similar experiences. The censorship of these narratives raises concerns about the suppression of diverse voices and the impact on those seeking representation and acceptance.

5

Facts of Life

Within the literary landscape, certain books confront the sensitive topics of sexual well-being, puberty, and consent head-on. These works aim to educate and empower readers, providing them with the essential knowledge to navigate their own bodies, relationships, and personal boundaries. However, the open discussion of such subjects often generates discomfort and controversy, resulting in censorship attempts and bans. We need to explore the societal impact of suppressing comprehensive sex education and examine books that have faced bans and challenges for their content.

"The Ruby Oliver Quartet" by E. Lockhart is a series of young adult novels that candidly explores the complexities of adolescence, relationships, and sexuality. Through the protagonist's experiences, the books address themes of consent, healthy relationships, and the challenges of puberty. Despite their potential to resonate with young readers and foster understanding, the series has encountered attempts at censorship due to its frank discussions of teenage sexuality.

"Sex, Puberty, and All That Stuff: A Guide to Growing Up" by Jacqui Bailey is a comprehensive guidebook designed to provide young readers with accurate information about growing up, including topics such as puberty, sexual health, and relationships. The book aims to empower young individuals by equipping them with the knowledge they need to make informed decisions and develop a positive attitude toward their bodies and sexuality. However, its direct approach to these subjects has led to bans in some places, with some deeming the content too explicit or inappropriate.

"It's Perfectly Normal" by Robie H. Harris is a highly regarded book that offers age-appropriate information about sexual health, emotional well-being, and relationships for children aged 10 and older. The book covers a range of topics, including puberty, pregnancy, sexual orientation, and consent. Despite its intention to provide inclusive and comprehensive education, it has faced bans in several jurisdictions due to its frank discussions of sex, which some find controversial or objectionable.

"Lawn Boy" by Jonathan Evison takes on the sensitive issue of sexual assault, portraying the story of a young man who experiences abuse by his employer. The book explores themes of power dynamics, consent, and the emotional repercussions of such traumatic experiences. While the intention is to shed light on an important issue and spark dialogue, it has been banned in certain places due to its explicit depiction of sex and sexual assault.

"The House on Mango Street" by Sandra Cisneros features Esperanza Cordero, a young Latina girl navigating life in Chicago. It's written as a series of vignettes touching on themes of identity,

gender roles, and poverty. Despite its literary acclaim, the book has been challenged or banned in some schools due to its explicit sexual content, mature themes like domestic abuse, and use of the Spanish language and Chicano dialect.

The suppression of books that address sexual well-being, puberty, and consent has far-reaching implications for young readers and society as a whole. By limiting access to accurate information and diverse perspectives, we hinder the development of a healthy understanding of one's body, healthy relationships, and consent. Comprehensive sex education plays a vital role in equipping young individuals with the necessary knowledge and skills to navigate their sexual journey, communicate effectively, and engage in consensual and respectful relationships.

The banning of books addressing these topics bolsters a culture of silence, shame, and misinformation. It denies young readers the opportunity to access valuable resources that can guide them toward a healthy understanding of their own bodies, establish boundaries, and make informed choices. By supporting the availability of these books, we promote a society that prioritizes sexual health, consent, and the well-being of all individuals.

6

Glass Ceilings

Books that illuminate the stories of remarkable women have the power to inspire, empower, and challenge societal norms. It is crucial to examine the censorship and challenges faced by books that highlight influential women and explore the feminist movement. However, some individuals and institutions view these books as threats to what they view as societal norms, fearing that they may disrupt traditional gender roles or promote ideas that go against conservative beliefs. As a result, these books face censorship, removal from libraries and curricula, and challenges from those who seek to maintain the dominance of male narratives and perspectives.

"Hidden Figures" by Margot Lee Shetterly is a compelling work that sheds light on the untold stories of African American female mathematicians who played pivotal roles at NASA during the space race. Despite the historical significance and inspirational nature of the book, it has been challenged and banned in certain educational settings. The objections often stem from the belief that the book

promotes ideas of racial and gender equality that some find uncomfortable or incompatible with their worldview.

"The Feminine Mystique" by Betty Friedan is a groundbreaking work that sparked the second-wave feminist movement. This book critically examines the traditional roles assigned to women in post-World War II America, challenging the notion that their fulfillment lies solely in domesticity. Its impact on the feminist discourse is undeniable, but it has faced bans and censorship for its perceived promotion of ideas that contradict traditional gender roles and challenge societal expectations.

"Our Bodies, Ourselves" by the Boston Women's Health Book Collective provides essential information about women's health and sexuality. It addresses topics such as contraception, abortion, and self-help medical care. Yet, due to its frank and comprehensive approach to women's reproductive health, the book has encountered challenges and bans from those who oppose its progressive stance on these issues.

"The Handmaid's Tale" by Margaret Atwood is a dystopian novel that envisions a society where women's rights and autonomy are severely restricted. It has also faced censorship. This thought-provoking work serves as a cautionary tale, but its exploration of reproductive rights and gender oppression has made it a target for censorship in some communities.

"Drum Dream Girl" by Margarita Engle is a book that challenges societal norms and celebrates the indomitable spirit of a young girl who dreams of playing the drums. It focuses on Millo Castro Zaldarriaga, a Chinese-African-Cuban girl who dares to break Cuba's

traditional taboo against female drummers. Through lyrical prose and vibrant illustrations, this banned book inspires readers to embrace their passions, break barriers, and defy expectations.

"At the Mountain's Base" by Traci Sorell weaves the tale of a Cherokee family separated by duty and distance. It illuminates the strength and resilience of a family as they wait anxiously for a loved one, a pilot, to return from war. It also celebrates the enduring spirit of Cherokee culture and the courage of history-making female pilots.

These books, which celebrate the achievements and struggles of women throughout history, have often been met with resistance and attempts to limit their accessibility. By taking a look at these bans, we can uncover the implications of perpetuating traditional gender roles and the negative consequences of silencing women's voices. It is vital to recognize the negative consequences of such censorship and strive for a society that embraces diverse perspectives and empowers all individuals, regardless of their gender.

The consequences of banning books that highlight influential women and examine the feminist movement are far-reaching. By limiting access to these texts, we not only erase the achievements and struggles of women but also continues harmful gender stereotypes and reinforce traditional roles assigned to women in society. Young readers are deprived of the opportunity to learn about diverse female role models, hindering their understanding of the importance of gender equality and the need for a more inclusive and equitable world.

By silencing these voices, we deny ourselves the chance to engage in critical discussions about gender equality, reproductive rights, and the dismantling of patriarchal structures. This fosters a cycle of ignorance and reinforces the marginalization of women's perspectives in public discourse.

7

Silencing the Struggles

Banned books that address mental health, suicide, and substance abuse shed light on important societal issues and personal struggles. Books addressing bullying tackle the experiences of those who have been marginalized or mistreated, offering valuable perspectives that promote empathy, discussions about respect and inclusion, and awareness of the impact. Unfortunately, these books frequently face bans and challenges due to concerns about their content and suitability.

"*We Are the Ants*" by Shaun David Hutchinson is a science fiction novel that centers around Henry, a teenage boy who grapples with depression and loss after his boyfriend's death by suicide. The book delves into themes of mental health, grief, and the search for meaning. It has faced bans and challenges due to its depiction of suicide and explicit language. However, it provides a candid and empathetic portrayal of the challenges faced by individuals dealing with mental health issues, promoting understanding and encouraging conversations about suicide prevention and support.

"13 Reasons Why" by Jay Asher is a bestselling novel that follows Clay Jensen as he listens to a series of tapes recorded by his classmate Hannah Baker before her suicide. It explores the reasons behind her decision and addresses issues such as bullying, sexual assault, and mental health. The book has faced significant controversy and censorship attempts due to concerns that it glamorizes suicide and fails to provide appropriate support or guidance for vulnerable readers. However, it serves as a catalyst for important discussions about the consequences of bullying, the impact of trauma, and the need for improved mental health resources in schools.

"Speak" by Laurie Halse Anderson is a novel that follows Melinda Sordino, a high school student who becomes an outcast after calling the police at a party. It tackles themes of trauma, depression, and the impact of sexual assault on mental health. It has been challenged and banned in some school districts due to its frank portrayal of sensitive topics and its explicit content. However, the book provides a powerful and necessary voice for survivors of sexual assault, encouraging dialogue, empathy, and the importance of speaking up against injustice.

"The Perks of Being a Wallflower" by Stephen Chbosky is a novel that presents a series of letters written by a boy named Charlie to an anonymous recipient, discussing his experiences, fears, and emotions. It's lauded for its heartfelt portrayal of adolescence, mental health, and the transition from childhood to adulthood. It was challenged and banned in some schools due to its discussion of topics like homosexuality, sexual activity, drug use, and incidents of mental illness and suicide.

"The Absolutely True Diary of a Part-Time Indian" by Sherman Alexie is a semi-autobiographical novel that chronicles the life of Arnold Spirit Jr., a Native American teenager living on a reservation. The book has been celebrated for its frank and sensitive discussion of issues faced by Native American communities. It has been banned or challenged in some areas due to its sexual content, offensive language, and depiction of alcohol.

"Looking for Alaska" by John Green is a novel that revolves around Miles Halter, who enrolls in a boarding school and forms deep connections with his classmates, particularly the enigmatic Alaska Young. It addresses themes of grief, self-destructive behavior, and the quest for meaning. The book has faced censorship attempts and bans for its depictions of sexual content, drug use, and offensive language. However, it offers a poignant examination of the complexities of adolescence, addressing topics such as grief, guilt, and the search for identity with sensitivity and thoughtfulness.

These books offer insights into the complexities of mental health, suicide, and substance abuse, providing readers with an opportunity to develop empathy, understanding, and awareness. Despite the controversies and challenges they have faced, they contribute to important conversations surrounding these issues. By engaging with these narratives, readers can gain valuable perspectives, foster empathy, and work towards creating a more compassionate and supportive society.

8

Whitewashing War

The world of banned books encompasses literary works that dare to question governmental authority, explore the realities of war, and challenge prevailing narratives surrounding violence. These texts provide powerful critiques of established systems and shed light on the complex and sometimes uncomfortable truths of human conflict. They offer readers an opportunity to delve into the multifaceted aspects of war, examining its consequences, ethical dilemmas, and the often-dehumanizing nature of violence. However, due to their controversial nature, these books have often become targets for censorship and attempts to suppress their voices.

"Catch-22" by Joseph Heller is a satirical novel set during World War II and offers a scathing examination of the absurdity and bureaucracy of war. Through the lens of the protagonist, Yossarian, Heller exposes the inherent contradictions and senselessness of military operations. The book challenges the notions of honor, duty, and sanity in the face of senseless violence. It has faced censorship attempts due to its strong language, sexual content, and anti-authoritarian themes. Nevertheless, it serves as a poignant commentary on the dehumanizing effects of war and the contradictions within military systems. By exposing the absurdities and illogicality of war, it prompts readers to question blind obedience and the consequences of unchecked power.

"*Slaughterhouse-Five*" by Kurt Vonnegut blends science fiction elements with a war narrative. This renowned novel follows the experiences of Billy Pilgrim, a World War II soldier who becomes "unstuck in time," traversing various moments of his life. Through this fragmented narrative, Vonnegut explores the horrors of war, the concept of free will, and the lingering trauma that follows soldiers long after the battles have ended. It has been banned and challenged due to its depictions of violence, sexual content, and perceived anti-war sentiment. However, the book offers a profound reflection on the human cost of war and the necessity of empathy and understanding. It challenges conventional notions of heroism and invites readers to confront the harsh realities of conflict.

"*For Whom the Bell Tolls*" by Ernest Hemingway transports readers to the Spanish Civil War, exploring themes of sacrifice, idealism, and the human toll of armed conflict. Through his vivid prose, Hemingway presents a nuanced portrayal of individuals grappling with loyalty, duty, and the complexities of war. It has faced challenges and bans due to its depictions of violence, sexual content, and political ideology. However, the book offers a poignant meditation on the universality of human suffering and the devastating impact of war on both individuals and societies.

"*The Naked and the Dead*" by Norman Mailer is set during World War II in the Pacific Theater. This novel offers a gritty and unflinching exploration of the experiences of soldiers in combat. Through vivid and often harrowing depictions, Mailer describes the psychological and physical toll of war on the human spirit. It has faced censorship attempts due to its language, sexual content, and graphic violence. Nevertheless, the book provides a searing critique of the dehumanization inherent in armed conflict and urges readers to consider the consequences of war beyond the glorified narratives often presented.

"The Things They Carried" by Tim O'Brien is a collection of interconnected stories that presents a haunting portrayal of the Vietnam War and its impact on soldiers. O'Brien blurs the line between fact and fiction, exploring the psychological burdens carried by soldiers and the unreliability of memory. This book has been both celebrated for its powerful depiction of war and targeted for censorship due to its language, sexual content, and depiction of violence. However, the book offers a profound exploration of the human experience in war, emphasizing the personal stories and internal struggles that often go unnoticed. By giving voice to the soldiers and their experiences, O'Brien challenges sanitized narratives of war and encourages readers to grapple with the complex emotional realities faced by those on the frontlines.

"All Quiet on the Western Front" by Erich Maria Remarque is set during World War I and follows the experiences of Paul Bäumer, a young German soldier. Through Paul's eyes, the book provides a stark and unflinching portrayal of the brutalities and futility of war. It has faced bans and challenges for its pacifist themes, anti-war sentiments, and depictions of graphic violence. However, the book offers an intimate examination of the human cost of war, challenging romanticized notions of heroism and shedding light on the

physical and psychological toll experienced by soldiers. Remarque's work serves as a powerful reminder of the tragedy and senselessness of war and the lasting impact it has on individuals and societies.

These books, among others, confront readers with the realities of armed conflict and its consequences. By challenging prevailing narratives and questioning the established authority, they provide a crucial opportunity for introspection, empathy, and a deeper understanding of the complexities of war. Censoring these works limits our ability to grapple with the profound human experiences of soldiers and undermines our capacity to critically examine the impact of violence on individuals and societies.

In the face of censorship, it is imperative to preserve and celebrate the voices that challenge the status quo and offer valuable insights into the true nature of war. As we reflect on the impact of banning books that question governmental authority, explore the realities of war, and challenge prevailing narratives surrounding violence, it becomes evident that limiting exposure to these narratives has profound implications for public opinion and democracy. When certain perspectives and critical examinations of power structures are silenced, the collective understanding of complex issues becomes narrower, and the opportunity for informed and inclusive dialogue diminishes.

By banning books that offer alternative viewpoints on war and violence, we risk perpetuating a sanitized and idealized version of history. Limiting access to these narratives prevents individuals from engaging with the nuanced complexities and ethical dilemmas inherent in armed conflict. It narrows our understanding of the consequences of war, the perspectives of those directly affected, and the potential lessons to be learned. Without the ability to critically analyze and challenge prevailing narratives, public opinion may become skewed, reinforcing notions of glorification or unquestioning support for military endeavors. It also hampers our ability to hold those in power accountable.

These books often shed light on the potential abuses of authority, the erosion of civil liberties, and the dangers of unchecked power. By silencing these voices, we create a society where dissent is suppressed and the mechanisms of democracy are undermined. An informed citizenry relies on access to diverse perspectives and a robust exchange of ideas. Banning books that challenge authority limits this exchange and stifles democratic discourse.

In a democratic society, the freedom to access diverse viewpoints and engage with controversial and challenging ideas is essential. To safeguard democracy, it is crucial to recognize the value of these narratives and advocate for the freedom of individuals to access and explore diverse perspectives. By embracing the power of literature to challenge prevailing narratives, we create space for dialogue, critical thinking, and a more comprehensive understanding of the world in which we live. It is through this engagement that we can work towards a more inclusive, empathetic, and informed society that upholds the principles of democracy.

9

Dangerous Acts of Learning

The suppression of books promoting critical thinking and intellectual growth is a concerning phenomenon that raises important questions about the long-term consequences of inhibiting the pursuit of knowledge. Throughout history, certain books have been targeted and suppressed due to their potential to challenge established beliefs, encourage critical analysis, and empower individuals to think independently. There is an inherent danger of impeding the act of learning and limiting intellectual growth.

These books often become the subject of censorship because they introduce ideas that challenge existing power structures, social norms, and ideological frameworks. These texts possess the potential to disrupt the status quo and encourage readers to question the world around them. By inhibiting access to such books, we deny individuals the opportunity to engage in independent thought, form their own opinions, and contribute to the development of a vibrant and intellectually diverse society.

"1984" by George Orwell is a dystopian novel that has faced numerous challenges and bans due to its critique of totalitarianism, government surveillance, and censorship. The book's exploration of themes such as thought control and manipulation poses a threat to those who wish to control information and limit dissent.

"Brave New World" by Aldous Huxley is another dystopian novel that has been subject to bans and challenges for its depiction of a society controlled by technology and the dehumanization of its citizens. Its examination of themes such as individual freedom, conformity, and the dangers of a utopian vision challenges the status quo and raises uncomfortable questions.

"The Catcher in the Rye" by J.D. Salinger is a classic novel about teenage angst and alienation that has frequently been targeted for censorship due to its profanity, sexual references, and portrayal of rebellious behavior. The book's frank and authentic depiction of adolescent struggles and disillusionment unsettles some individuals who prefer to shield young readers from such realities.

"The Adventures of Huckleberry Finn" by Mark Twain is a seminal novel that has faced bans and challenges due to its use of racial slurs and its exploration of racism and societal hypocrisy. The book's unflinching portrayal of the realities of race relations and its commentary on the moral failings of society has made it a target for censorship, despite its historical and literary significance.

"The Handmaid's Tale" by Margaret Atwood is a dystopian novel set in a totalitarian society where women are oppressed and controlled. It has faced challenges and bans for its exploration of themes such as feminism, reproductive rights, and religious extremism. Its critique of gender roles and its depiction of a future where women's rights are curtailed make it a target for censorship by those who fear its social and political implications.

"The Scarlet Letter" by Nathaniel Hawthorne is a classic novel about adultery and the moral hypocrisy of Puritan society. It has been the subject of bans and challenges for its sexual content and perceived immorality. The book's examination of guilt, sin, and societal judgment raises uncomfortable questions about human nature and societal norms.

"The Hunger Games" by Suzanne Collins is a popular young adult dystopian series that has faced bans and challenges for its depictions of violence, political oppression, and rebellion. The book's exploration of themes such as power, inequality, and the exploitation of youth resonates with readers but has also drawn criticism from those who deem it inappropriate for young audiences.

"Call of the Wild" by Jack London is an adventure novel by Jack London. It is set in the Yukon, Canada during the 1890s Klondike Gold Rush, a period when strong sled dogs were in high demand. The novel's central character is a dog named Buck, a domesticated pet who is stolen from his home in California and sold into service as a sled dog in Alaska. The book chronicles Buck's struggle for survival and his rise to become the leader of a wolf pack. While it's considered a classic of American literature, it has been challenged and even banned in some places due to the depiction of violence and

cruelty to animals, which some readers find disturbing. In addition, the harsh realities of life and death depicted in the book have been deemed too intense for younger readers by some schools and libraries. The book's perceived racial undertones have also contributed to its controversy. It continues to be both celebrated for its literary merits and scrutinized for its content.

The act of learning is a fundamental aspect of human growth and progress. It allows us to expand our understanding, challenge preconceived notions, and cultivate empathy and compassion. By suppressing books that foster critical thinking, we stifle intellectual curiosity and hinder the development of well-rounded individuals capable of engaging in informed and meaningful discussions.

One of the key long-term consequences of inhibiting intellectual growth is the perpetuation of ignorance and the potential for manipulation. When certain ideas and perspectives are suppressed, individuals are deprived of the opportunity to engage with alternative viewpoints, assess evidence critically, and make informed decisions. This lack of exposure to diverse ideas leaves individuals vulnerable to manipulation and propaganda, as they are denied the tools necessary to discern fact from fiction and think critically about the information they encounter.

Limiting intellectual growth has broader societal implications. It hinders progress in fields such as science, technology, and social justice, as the exploration of new ideas and the challenging of established paradigms are essential for innovation and positive change. When books promoting critical thinking are banned or restricted, we risk stifling creativity, innovation, and the advancement of society as a whole.

In a democratic society, the freedom to access a wide range of ideas and engage in critical discourse is vital. Banning or suppressing books that encourage critical thinking undermines the very foundation of intellectual freedom and inhibits the development of an informed and engaged citizenry. It is through the exploration of diverse perspectives and the challenging of established knowledge that societies evolve, address systemic issues, and strive for a more just and equitable world.

By promoting intellectual growth and embracing books that foster critical thinking, we can cultivate a society that values open dialogue, diversity of thought, and the pursuit of knowledge. It is through these endeavors that we can break free from the constraints of ignorance and build a future that is grounded in understanding, empathy, and progress. The suppression of such works hampers intellectual growth, inhibits societal progress, and threatens the very foundation of a free and democratic society.

10

Sacred Censorship

Religious beliefs and practices hold significant influence over individuals and communities, shaping their values, morals, and worldview. However, when it comes to literature that discusses religiously controversial topics or offers alternative perspectives on faith, conflicts arise between the principles of freedom of religion and freedom of speech.

"The Satanic Verses" by Salman Rushdie is a novel that ignited intense controversy and faced widespread bans due to its exploration of Islamic themes. The book discusses the complex intertwining of religion, identity, and cultural heritage. Rushdie's narrative reimagines and reinterprets historical events, including the concept of the "satanic verses" from early Islamic history. These reinterpretations, along with other elements of the story, were deemed offensive and sacrilegious by certain segments of the Muslim community. The controversy resulted in a call for Rushdie's death issued by Ayatollah Ruhollah Khomeini, the Supreme Leader of Iran at the time. The

call led to threats, violence, and even the assassination of translators and publishers associated with the book.

"*The Da Vinci Code*" by Dan Brown is a bestselling thriller that weaves together art, history, and religious symbolism. The novel explores a fictional narrative surrounding the Holy Grail, Jesus Christ, and the role of secret societies within Christianity. Brown's book challenges established narratives and offers alternative interpretations of religious history and doctrine. It faced significant backlash from certain religious groups who found its narrative deeply troubling and offensive to their beliefs.

Religious texts themselves have not been immune to challenges and bans. Even the widely revered "*The Bible*" has faced temporary bans in certain contexts. In some instances, parents have objected to the inclusion of the Bible in school curricula or libraries, citing concerns about its content, such as perceived sexual content, vulgarity, or violence. Similar challenges have been made against other religious texts such as "*The Quran*" and "*The Book of Mormon*."

The "*Harry Potter*" series by J.K. Rowling follows the story of a young wizard, Harry Potter, and his friends Hermione Granger and Ron Weasley, all of whom are students at Hogwarts School of Witchcraft and Wizardry. The main story arc concerns Harry's struggle against the dark wizard Lord Voldemort, who aims to become immortal and subjugate all wizards and Muggles (non-magical people). Despite its popularity and influence, the series has been frequently challenged and banned in certain regions, often by groups who claim that the books promote witchcraft and the occult, which they believe is contrary to their religious beliefs.

"Bridge to Terabithia" by Katherine Paterson tells the story of Jesse Aarons and Leslie Burke, two fifth graders who create an imaginary kingdom in the woods called Terabithia. The novel explores themes of friendship, imagination, and dealing with tragedy. Some critics have banned or challenged the book, alleging that it promotes secular humanism, New Age religion, occultism, and Satanism. These critics often take issue with the use of fantasy and the notion of an imaginary, god-like figure in Terabithia.

"A Wrinkle in Time" by Madeleine L'Engle is a science fantasy novel about Meg Murry, a high-school-aged girl who is transported on an adventure through time and space with her younger brother Charles Wallace and her friend Calvin O'Keefe to rescue her father, a gifted scientist, from the evil forces that hold him prisoner on another planet. The book has faced bans and challenges from critics who believe it incorporates elements of witchcraft and occultism. Some also argue that the book challenges religious beliefs, due to L'Engle's combination of science and religion and her portrayal of God as encompassing all good things, which conflicts with some traditional religious views.

"The Berenstain Bears and the Big Question" by Stan Berenstain and Jan Berenstain is an installment of the classic Berenstain Bears series. Sister Bear grapples with understanding who God is and His presence in the world. Her curiosity is met with guidance from Papa and Mama Bear, who teach her to recognize God's blessings in everything from the sunshine to the birds and even in their chapel. Despite its attempt to teach children about spirituality and divine presence, the book has been challenged and banned. The controversy typically stems from differing opinions on the appropriateness

of discussing religious topics in children's literature, especially in settings like schools.

"The Gift of Ramadan" by Rabiah York Lumbard is about Sophia, the young protagonist of this family-centric tale, who is eager to observe Ramadan by fasting, attracted by her grandma's description of fasting making a person "sparkly." However, when her efforts to fast don't work out, Sophia discovers alternative ways to participate in the Ramadan holiday. This engaging story, which explores the diversity of practices during Ramadan, has faced challenges and bans. These are typically due to the inclusion of religious content.

"Fahrenheit 451" by Ray Bradbury is a dystopian novel set in a future society that prohibits books, employing "firemen" like the protagonist, Guy Montag, to burn any discovered volumes. Montag eventually rebels against this societal norm, leaving his job to join a group that memorizes and circulates globally significant literature. Despite its anti-censorship themes, it has been ironically banned and challenged for its strong language, violent content, and negative depiction of religion, with critics citing these elements as unsuitable for certain audiences.

These objections highlight the tension between protecting religious beliefs and maintaining freedom of speech. These texts hold profound significance for their respective religious communities, and their censorship raises important questions about the balance between religious reverence and the free exchange of ideas.

The conflict between religious beliefs and freedom of speech is a complex and nuanced issue, as it involves balancing the rights and sensitivities of individuals and communities. While religious texts hold deep significance for many, it is important to recognize that diverse perspectives exist and that the freedom to express and examine those perspectives is a fundamental aspect of a democratic society.

It is crucial to foster an environment where open discussions about religion and religious texts can take place, even when those discussions may challenge prevailing beliefs or provoke discomfort. The suppression of religiously controversial books not only limits intellectual exploration but also hinders the potential for mutual understanding, growth, and dialogue among individuals from different religious backgrounds.

In navigating the delicate balance between freedom of religion and freedom of speech, it is essential to protect the right to express diverse beliefs and viewpoints while also respecting the right of individuals to hold and practice their religious faith. By fostering an environment that encourages open-mindedness, critical thinking, and respectful dialogue, we can engage with religiously sensitive topics in a way that promotes understanding, tolerance, and the advancement of knowledge. By recognizing the significance of freedom of speech and the need for respectful engagement with diverse perspectives, we can foster a society that embraces intellectual curiosity and nurtures an environment conducive to religious understanding and harmony.

11

The Wealth of Ignorance

We now turn our attention to works that tackle the subject of income inequality and expose the flaws of capitalism. These books offer critical perspectives that challenge prevailing narratives and shed light on the systemic issues that contribute to economic disparities. These have faced challenges and objections in various contexts due to their provocative content and potential to disrupt the status quo.

"The Working Poor: Invisible in America" by David K. Shipler is a compelling examination of poverty in the United States, revealing the struggles and hardships faced by individuals and families living on the fringes of society. Through vivid personal narratives and meticulous research, Shipler exposes the structural factors that uphold poverty and the barriers that prevent upward mobility. Some argue that the book challenges the dominant narrative that places sole responsibility for poverty on individual choices, instead highlighting the systemic forces at play. Its unflinching portrayal of

poverty and the failures of the economic system has unsettled those who prefer to maintain the illusion of a meritocratic society.

"Nickel and Dimed: On (Not) Getting By in America" by Barbara Ehrenreich takes readers on an immersive journey as Barbara Ehrenreich delves into low-wage jobs to expose the challenges faced by the working poor. Through her firsthand experiences, she shines a light on the daily struggles, meager wages, and systemic issues that perpetuate poverty in America. Despite its aim to spark dialogue and raise awareness about the difficulties faced by low-wage workers, it has faced objections and restrictions in certain educational settings. The book challenges the myth of upward mobility and forces readers to confront the harsh realities of inadequate wages and precarious employment. Its critique of capitalism and exploration of income inequality may have made it a target for those who seek to protect the economic status quo.

"The Grapes of Wrath" by John Steinbeck is a powerful novel depicting the struggles of migrant workers during the Great Depression that has encountered censorship attempts due to its social and political themes. Steinbeck's critique of capitalism, social inequality, and the exploitation of labor has made the book a lightning rod for those who seek to suppress narratives that challenge the prevailing economic and social structures.

The banning or attempted suppression of books that address income inequality and criticize the flaws of capitalism raises significant concerns about the restriction of knowledge and the stifling of critical perspectives. By silencing these narratives, we risk perpetuating ignorance about the lived experiences of marginalized communities and impeding the necessary dialogue for social and economic progress.

These books provide valuable insights into the struggles faced by individuals in economically disadvantaged positions and offer a deeper understanding of the systemic issues that foster income inequality. They encourage readers to critically examine the structures and ideologies that shape our economic systems and consider alternative approaches to promote greater equity and justice. It is vital to recognize the importance of intellectual freedom, diverse viewpoints, and informed public discourse. By engaging with these works, we can foster a more nuanced understanding of economic challenges, challenge existing power structures, and strive toward a more inclusive and equitable society.

12

The Cost of Banning Books

It is essential to confront the inherent hypocrisy embedded within laws and policies that aim to impose one side's religious ideology on every parent and restrict what children can read. By allowing such restrictions, we raise a crucial question: What if the roles were reversed?

Imagine a scenario where a different set of religious beliefs held the dominant position, and their ideologies were the ones dictating what books were acceptable for children. Those who champion the current bans and restrictions might find themselves at odds with such impositions, advocating for their right to choose what their children are exposed to and what aligns with their own beliefs.

The freedom to choose what our children read and learn is a deeply personal matter, one that should rest in the hands of the parents themselves. Each family holds unique values, cultural backgrounds, and religious beliefs, and it is within this diversity that the richness of our society thrives. By upholding the right of parents to make informed decisions about their children's education, we foster a sense of respect for individual autonomy and the diversity of our communities.

The principle of parental rights cannot be understated. Parents are best positioned to understand their children's needs, beliefs, and sensitivities. They have the wisdom and insight to navigate their children's intellectual development in a manner that aligns with their own values and supports their growth. Placing this responsibility solely in the hands of external entities or rigid governmental policies undermines the crucial role that parents play in shaping their children's education and worldview.

By acknowledging the importance of parental rights, we honor the diverse perspectives and belief systems that exist within our society. We recognize that the responsibility of guiding children's literary choices rests with the parents, who can foster critical thinking, open dialogue, and the development of values that align with their own families' moral compass. This approach respects the rights of all families, regardless of their beliefs or backgrounds, and promotes an inclusive and democratic society that upholds the principles of individual liberty and personal choice.

Let us not succumb to the fallacy of assuming that a singular ideology can dictate what is appropriate for all children. Instead, let us embrace the notion that a pluralistic society thrives when we respect the rights and autonomy of individual families. By allowing parents to make decisions regarding their children's reading materials, we empower them to foster an environment that is conducive to their children's well-being, growth, and moral development. It encourages a society that values critical thinking, open dialogue, and the exploration of various ideas and perspectives. Let us strive for a world where every parent is empowered to make informed decisions for their children, where intellectual freedom is cherished, and where the hypocrisy of attempting to control children's reading choices is laid to rest.

At the heart of this discussion lies the importance of freedom of speech as a fundamental pillar of democratic societies. It is through this cherished freedom that we enable the exchange of ideas, the pursuit of truth, and the growth of knowledge. The act of banning books directly undermines this cornerstone of democracy, suffocating the free flow of ideas and impeding the exploration of diverse perspectives.

When books are banned, voices are silenced, and with them, opportunities for dialogue, understanding, and progress are lost. By suppressing certain ideas and narratives, we inadvertently create an environment of ignorance and conformity. We deny individuals the right to engage with a wide range of perspectives, hindering their ability to form independent opinions and make informed decisions. In essence, book bans limit the very essence of what it means to be an informed and engaged citizen.

This book serves as a poignant reminder of the paradox we face when contemplating censorship. By censoring a book that challenges the status quo, we inadvertently underscore the need for its existence. We highlight the power of literature to provoke thought, spark discussions, and challenge societal norms. The irony lies in the fact that the act of banning a book only amplifies its significance and the urgency to read it.

By banning any book, we risk denying ourselves the opportunity to confront uncomfortable realities and grapple with complex issues. We limit the scope of public discourse and hinder the transformative power of literature in fostering empathy and understanding. The cost of this suppression extends beyond the pages of the banned book—it infiltrates our collective consciousness, distorting our understanding of the world and hindering our capacity for growth.

Banning a book not only limits access to knowledge but also diminishes the richness of our cultural heritage. Literature serves as a reflection of the human experience, capturing the complexities of our world, our history, and our aspirations. Banned books often tackle important and sensitive topics, shedding light on social injustices, historical atrocities, and the struggles of marginalized communities. By suppressing these narratives, we risk erasing important aspects of our collective memory and perpetuating historical ignorance.

As we contemplate the cost of banning a book, we must recognize the vital role that freedom of speech plays in our lives. It is through the free exchange of ideas, even those that challenge prevailing norms, that societies have the opportunity to grow, adapt, and address the pressing issues of our time. The suppression of speech restricts our capacity to understand and address the complexities of our world and hinders the pursuit of justice, equality, and progress.

We need to embrace the power of literature, challenge censorship, and advocate for the right to read. By doing so, we create a society that fosters intellectual growth, celebrates diverse perspectives, and upholds the principles of democracy.

13

Between Dogma and Power

If you think the things I have said so far are controversial, you should probably put this book down because I am about to make you really uncomfortable with some hard truths. What we now have to realize is that it's not just about book bans, is it? They are intertwined with broader societal trends aimed at maintaining control and perpetuating systemic inequalities. There is an intricate web that connects the banning of books to the neverending fight against welfare programs, public schools, higher education, universal healthcare, and reproductive rights.

At the heart of this suppression lies a fear of knowledge and independent thought. By limiting access to higher education, these groups seek to keep individuals uninformed and less equipped to critically examine social structures and power dynamics. They exploit the vulnerability of the uneducated, using religion as a tool to control and manipulate, discouraging questioning and stifling curiosity. By controlling education, these groups can shape the beliefs and values of the next generation, ensuring the perpetuation of their own agendas.

The argument for free higher education is rooted in the belief that it's an investment that can lead to substantial societal benefits. It promotes social equity by allowing individuals from all economic backgrounds equal access to higher education, thereby reducing income inequality over time. An educated workforce is often more productive and innovative, which can drive economic growth and competitiveness. Additionally, free higher education could help alleviate the burgeoning student debt crisis, enabling graduates to contribute to the economy sooner and without the burden of significant debt. The truth is that greater levels of education are associated with increased civic participation, leading to a more robust and engaged democracy. While there are fiscal implications, advocates argue that the long-term societal and economic returns far outweigh the costs.

The fight against comprehensive education, including efforts to limit access and deny free educational opportunities, further entrenches systemic inequalities. It is no coincidence that statistics show a correlation between education levels and voting patterns. An educated populace is less susceptible to manipulation, more capable of critical thinking, and less likely to adhere unquestioningly to dogmatic beliefs. By impeding access to education, these groups maintain power by keeping individuals uneducated and uninformed.

Recently. this has expanded beyond just schools and public libraries. Governor Ron DeSantis of Florida recently signed into law a series of higher education reforms, prohibiting colleges and universities in the state from spending on the majority of diversity, equity, and inclusion (DEI) programs. According to DeSantis, these programs propagate "woke" ideology, a claim that has drawn criticism from academics and Democrats who view this action as a violation of academic freedom and a potential deterrent to student and faculty recruitment and retention.

The difficult question becomes "Why?" This expansion of bans goes beyond protecting our children, we are now suppressing the knowledge from adults. The banning of books is about controlling the narratives. They are used as tools of ideological influence. Understanding this requires us to confront the disturbing parallels that exist between such ideologies.

The power of education and the shaping of young minds have long been recognized as pivotal in influencing the trajectory of societies. Extremist religious groups and ideologies are well aware of this fact. By controlling what children read, learn, and are exposed to, these groups attempt to mold the minds of the next generation according to their own beliefs and agendas. They recognize that by limiting access to certain ideas, narratives, and perspectives, they can manipulate the development of critical thinking and foster an environment that aligns with their own ideologies.

We must also address the ties between book bans and the fight against universal healthcare and reproductive rights. Access to healthcare, including reproductive healthcare, is a fundamental aspect of individual autonomy and well-being. By restricting these rights and limiting access to contraception and safe abortion services, individuals, particularly those from marginalized communities, are denied the ability to plan their futures, pursue education, and break free from the cycle of poverty. The control exerted through these measures not only impacts individuals' physical and mental health but also curtails their opportunities for personal and educational growth.

The interconnectedness of these various elements is alarming. These tools of suppression work in concert to continue a system of control. They reinforce existing power structures, keep individuals in a state of dependence, and hinder social progress.

The desire to keep the youth uneducated and shielded from alternative viewpoints stems from a fear of losing control and influence over future generations. These extremist groups understand that knowledge is power, and an informed and critically thinking youth poses a threat to their agendas. By suppressing intellectual exploration and exposure to diverse perspectives, they aim to maintain a stranglehold on the minds of young individuals, perpetuating a cycle of conformity and reinforcing their own power structures.

This reality raises profound concerns about the erosion of individual autonomy, the stifling of free thought, and the potential for a society driven by narrow-mindedness and intolerance. When we witness attempts to ban books that depict our difficult history, challenge established beliefs or shed light on uncomfortable truths, we are witnessing an insidious effort to shape the narrative, manipulate perception, and limit the potential for societal progress.

We must resist the manipulation of young minds and champion the importance of diverse knowledge, critical thinking, and the exploration of different perspectives. In doing so, we empower the youth to become active participants in shaping a future that is rooted in understanding, compassion, and informed decision-making.

The battle against book banning and the suppression of knowledge is not merely a fight for the freedom to read; it is a fight for the future of our societies. It is a call to reject the dangerous ideologies that seek to control young minds and embrace the principles of intellectual freedom, individual autonomy, and the pursuit of truth. By nurturing a generation of independent thinkers, equipped with knowledge, empathy, and the ability to critically analyze information, we can create a world that is resilient against the forces of ignorance and intolerance.

Throughout history, religious groups and certain political factions, particularly conservative or right-wing movements, have often shown a tendency to support book bans and oppose comprehensive education. While it is important to note that not all religious groups or Republicans advocate for such actions, it is worth examining the underlying motivations behind some of these efforts.

By restricting access to education, particularly comprehensive and critical education that promotes independent thinking and a deep understanding of complex issues, religious groups, and certain political factions can maintain control over their followers or supporters. They can support a cycle of poverty and limited opportunity that hinders social mobility and keeps certain segments of society marginalized and dependent on their ideological messages.

Similarly, political factions may seek to control information and limit education in order to maintain their power base. This can be seen in attempts to restrict access to comprehensive sex education or teachings on topics such as evolution or climate change. By keeping people uninformed or misinformed, these groups can shape public opinion and advance their own agendas.

Statistics show a correlation between education levels and political leanings. Research has consistently demonstrated that higher levels of education are associated with a greater likelihood of supporting progressive policies and voting for more liberal candidates. Educated individuals tend to have a broader worldview, value critical thinking, and are more open to diverse perspectives. On the other hand, those with lower levels of education may be more susceptible to manipulation, misinformation, and appeals to fear or prejudice. This can create a cycle of poverty and disenfranchisement, as individuals who lack educational opportunities may struggle to escape socioeconomic constraints.

However, it is essential to note that education is not a panacea for all societal challenges, and political beliefs are influenced by a multitude of factors beyond education alone. Individuals can hold diverse perspectives and make informed choices regardless of their educational background. It is important not to generalize or stereotype entire religious or political groups based on the actions of a few.

Throughout history, religion has played a significant role in shaping societies, moral codes, and belief systems. It has provided comfort, guidance, and a sense of purpose for countless individuals. However, when wielded as a tool for control, it can become a potent force in suppressing intellectual growth, fostering ignorance, and continuing inequality. The historical truth is that religion has been utilized to control the uneducated and discourage critical thinking, often serving as a barrier to progress and enlightenment.

One of the ways in which religious institutions exert control is by discouraging the exploration of scientific knowledge. By presenting certain scientific theories or discoveries as incompatible with religious doctrine, they instill doubt and skepticism, effectively discouraging believers from engaging with scientific concepts. This deliberate suppression of scientific education restricts the growth of knowledge and inhibits the potential for scientific advancements. This manipulation of religious beliefs to dismiss or deny established scientific facts not only hinders individual intellectual development but also impedes societal progress.

The trial of Galileo Galilei in the 17th century is a poignant illustration of the conflict between religious authority and scientific inquiry. Galileo supported heliocentrism, the theory that the Earth revolves around the Sun. This conflicted with the Catholic Church's geocentric view, that the Earth was the center of the universe, resulting in his condemnation by the Catholic Church.

Giordano Bruno was a philosopher and mathematician who lived during the 16th century. He proposed that the stars were distant suns surrounded by their own planets and might foster life of their own. He also insisted that the universe was infinite, which contradicted the religious beliefs of an Earth-centric universe. Bruno was eventually arrested by the Inquisition and burned at the stake for his heretical ideas.

Known as the Scopes Monkey Trial, this legal case in 1925 involved a high school teacher, John T. Scopes, who was accused of violating Tennessee's Butler Act which made it unlawful to teach human evolution in any state-funded school. The trial represented a fundamentalist reaction to the scientific theory of evolution and marked a pivotal moment in the conflict between science and religion in America.

Scientific understanding of gender and sexual orientation has evolved considerably, but some religious groups refuse to accept these findings. They argue that being LGBTQ+ is a choice or can be "cured," beliefs that go against the consensus in the scientific community.

The control exerted by religious ideologies extends beyond just science. It often intersects with issues such as reproductive rights, where bans on abortion disproportionately affect the poor and un-educated. Religious institutions and conservative groups often advocate for strict abortion laws based on religious beliefs, claiming to protect the sanctity of life. However, these bans disproportionately impact those who may lack access to comprehensive sex education, healthcare, and family planning resources. The result is a cycle of poverty and limited opportunities, perpetuated by policies that restrict reproductive autonomy and limit access to employment, education, and resources.

By keeping the uneducated confined within narrow ideological boundaries, those in positions of power can continue their influence and manipulate the narrative to serve their own interests. This manipulation is not limited to a specific religion or historical period but is a recurring theme in the dynamics between religious institutions, education, and power.

To break free from this cycle of control and suppression, it is important to promote a robust educational system that encourages critical thinking, scientific literacy, and the exploration of diverse perspectives. Education should empower individuals to question prevailing beliefs, engage in rigorous intellectual inquiry, and foster an appreciation for evidence-based knowledge. By equipping individuals with the tools to think independently and critically, we can counter the influence of manipulative ideologies and cultivate a society that values intellectual freedom and the pursuit of truth.

In recognizing the historical and present-day consequences of religious control over education, we must strive for a society that values both religious freedom and the right to intellectual exploration. By nurturing an environment that encourages dialogue, diversity of thought, and the pursuit of knowledge, we can transcend the limitations imposed by religious dogma and create a future that embraces the full potential of human intellect and fosters a more equitable and enlightened society.

Just as religious ideologies have been used historically to restrict access to certain knowledge and shape societal narratives, book bans serve as a tool to reinforce ignorance, maintain power structures, and restrict the free flow of ideas. Book bans are a manifestation of the fear and insecurity that arises when established beliefs and power structures are challenged. Whether it is books that explore sensitive topics such as sexuality, race, mental health, or religion, they become targets for censorship because they disrupt the established order and force us to confront unpleasant facts.

The consequences of book bans are far-reaching and detrimental. When we deny individuals access to diverse perspectives, controversial ideas, and uncomfortable histories, we inhibit their intellectual growth, stifle their thinking, and limit their capacity to engage with complex societal issues. We deny ourselves the opportunity to grapple with challenging concepts, expand our empathy, and gain a deeper understanding of the world around us.

Book bans also reinforce existing inequalities and encourage systemic oppression. We have seen how bans on books addressing issues of race, gender, and sexuality disproportionately impact marginalized communities, further muting their voices and experiences. By silencing these voices, we deny individuals the opportunity to see themselves represented in literature and to engage with stories that reflect their own struggles and aspirations. This erasure maintains societal divisions and denies us the opportunity to foster empathy, understanding, and solidarity.

The truth is that the act of book banning is inherently contradictory. Those who advocate for book bans in the name of protecting children, preserving religious values, or maintaining societal norms often fail to recognize the irony of their actions. In their attempt to shield individuals from challenging ideas, they undermine the very principles of intellectual freedom, free expression, and open dialogue that form the foundation of a democratic society that their freedom to practice their religion is founded on.

In an increasingly interconnected and diverse world, it is essential that we embrace the richness of ideas, engage in respectful dialogue, and challenge our own beliefs and biases. By promoting intellectual freedom and rejecting book bans, we create an environment where individuals are empowered to think critically, explore different perspectives, and navigate the complexities of our shared humanity.

As we reflect on the cumulative impact of book bans, we are reminded of the urgent need to defend intellectual freedom, challenge oppressive ideologies, and resist the forces that seek to limit our access to knowledge and shape our collective understanding. We must recognize that true intellectual growth and societal progress come from engaging with diverse perspectives, confronting harsh realities, and fostering an inclusive and open-minded society.

Book bans are not merely about the restriction of certain books. They represent a larger battle for intellectual freedom and the right to explore the full spectrum of human knowledge and experiences. By rejecting book bans and advocating for a society that embraces intellectual freedom, we can dismantle the barriers that hinder our collective growth, amplify marginalized voices, and create a future that celebrates the transformative power of literature, ideas, and the unyielding human spirit.

14

A Call to Action

The fight against book censorship is not a passive endeavor. It requires engagement, action, and persistence. So, what can you do about it?

First, stay informed. Familiarize yourself with the books frequently targeted for censorship and the reasons given for their bans. Read these books, understand their context, and form your own opinions. Knowledge is power, and your ability to argue against a book ban will be strengthened if you're familiar with the content.

Be vocal about your support for intellectual freedom. Write to local newspapers, blog about it, or share information on social media. Talk to friends, family, and community members about the importance of preserving diverse literary voices.

Engage with your local libraries and schools. Attend board meetings where decisions about book bans might be made. Stand up against efforts to ban books, and express your concerns about how such bans limit education and freedom of thought. Join or support organizations that fight against book censorship, like the American Library Association or the National Coalition Against Censorship. These groups often lead the charge in advocating for intellectual freedom and can provide resources and strategies to combat censorship. I provide a list of such organizations and links at the end of this book.

Support authors and publishers who are frequently targeted by book bans. Buying their books sends a message to those attempting to suppress these voices that their work is valuable and necessary.

Foster a culture of openness and respect for differing views. The fear of differing opinions often underlies book bans. By engaging in respectful, open conversations about controversial topics, you help normalize these discussions, reducing the perceived need for censorship.

Contact your community leaders and elected officials at every level. Make calls, send emails and letters to let them know that you do not support such bans and attacks on freedom of speech.

Most importantly, you need to vote. Vote in every election. As we have seen, elections have consequences and your vote is your voice. Make sure it is heard.

Remember, every voice counts in the battle against book censorship. It is not the responsibility of a single individual or organization but a collective effort made by us all. Your actions, no matter how small they may seem, can make a significant difference in safeguarding intellectual freedom and promoting a diverse, inclusive literary landscape. It's time for us all to stand up and protect our right to read.

15

Special Thanks

The individuals and entities listed below are staunch advocates for freedom of expression and fervent opponents of book censorship. Many of these sights also have links to banned books.

Marty Dodson - Instagram for banned Children's books.
instagram.com/martydsongs
amazon.com/shop/martydsongs/list/1CAIG6LC9XCZ6
PEN America
pen.org/
The American Library Association
ala.org/advocacy/bbooks
The American Civil Liberties Union (ACLU)
aclu.org/issues/free-speech
Amnesty International
amnesty.org/en/what-we-do/freedom-of-expression/
Banned Books Week Coalition
bannedbooksweek.org/
instagram.com/banned_books_week/

Comic Book Legal Defense Fund

cbldf.org/

Committee to Protect Journalists

cpj.org/

FreeMuse

Freemuse.org

Index on Censorship

indexoncensorship.org/

National Coalition Against Censorship

ncac.org/topic/internet-censorship

About The Author

Cara Cusack is a multifaceted author, IT Business Leader, mother, grandmother, and small-scale farmer. Born and raised in Texas, she now calls the beautiful landscapes of Washington State home. With an impressive 25-year career in information technology, Cara's wealth of knowledge is as broad as the landscapes she has traversed, from the green fields of Ireland to the coastal beauty of Malta and the rich jungles of Costa Rica.

While her career initially revolved around the dynamic field of IT, Cara's talents and passions have always stretched beyond the professional realm. She has always found joy in putting pen to paper, but it was a deep-seated belief in freedom of speech that transformed this hobby into a calling. In response to disturbing trends of book bans in schools and public libraries, Cara became determined to share her own voice and began to publish her writings.

Cara's repertoire of work is diverse, ranging from engaging children's stories to compelling fiction and non-fiction for adults. Her belief in diversity, inclusivity, and freedom of expression is often reflected in her work, though she also delights in creating purely fun, imaginative tales. The minds of her children and grandchildren serve as a constant source of inspiration, leading to a medley of stories that are as brilliant and creative as the young minds that helped spark them.

Whether she's penning an insightful piece of non-fiction or spinning a whimsical tale for children, Cara is driven by a love of literature and a commitment to ensuring the freedom and diversity of voices in the literary world. Her array of life experiences, coupled with her professional expertise, imbue her writing with a unique authenticity, making her a celebrated author and a beacon of freedom in literature.

Learn more at CaraCusackBooks.com

Printed in the USA
CPSIA information can be obtained
at www.ICGtesting.com
LVHW011320160823
755279LV00018BA/1228

9 781088 208663